(25) years of
Love &
Happiness

By Stu & Stephanie Halfacre

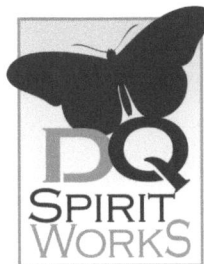

DQ SPIRIT WORKS

25 years of
Love & Happiness

Published by

DQ Spirit Works, LLC

ISBN-13: 978-0-9863588-3-8

First American Paperback Edition

Printed in the United States of America

Contents

On the cover:
Engagement photo

Once Upon A Long Ago...

Stu's perspective

In early 1993 I was living the life... so I thought. I had a house, a car (a gold Renault Alliance), a job as an art director and a dog (Corey) — but what more did I need to survive? Some said I was a guy who needed to get a life, but for me this was life. As a true loner, I was mostly content with making it on my own but there was also a part of me that desired a partner to travel life's journey. Unbeknown to me, my life as I knew it was about to be transformed into something beyond my everyday reality.

Steph's perspective

I have always looked forward to a New Year with great expectation that something good is going to happen. In the year of 1993 I was content, life was going great. I lived in a nice ranch style house, my car was in great shape with low mileage. I had been on a new job for almost two months. My girls were all in school and doing well. What more could I ask for; God had met my needs and I was making plans to go to Europe in March to visit my brother Mark and his family. I was very comfortable in who I was as a woman and a mother. My faith in God left me not wanting for anything. However, I had no idea what was about to happen in the coming days, months and years ahead.

My Reality
This was my life in early 1993.

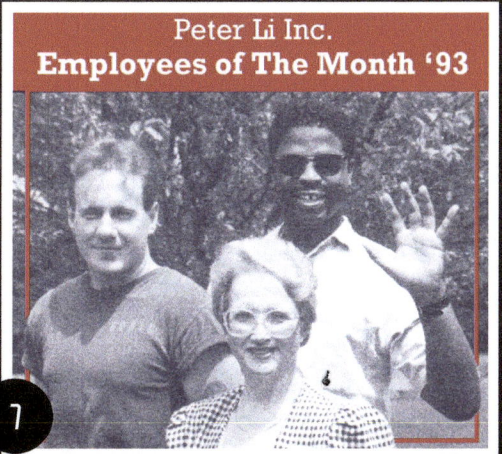

Peter Li Inc.
Employees of The Month '93

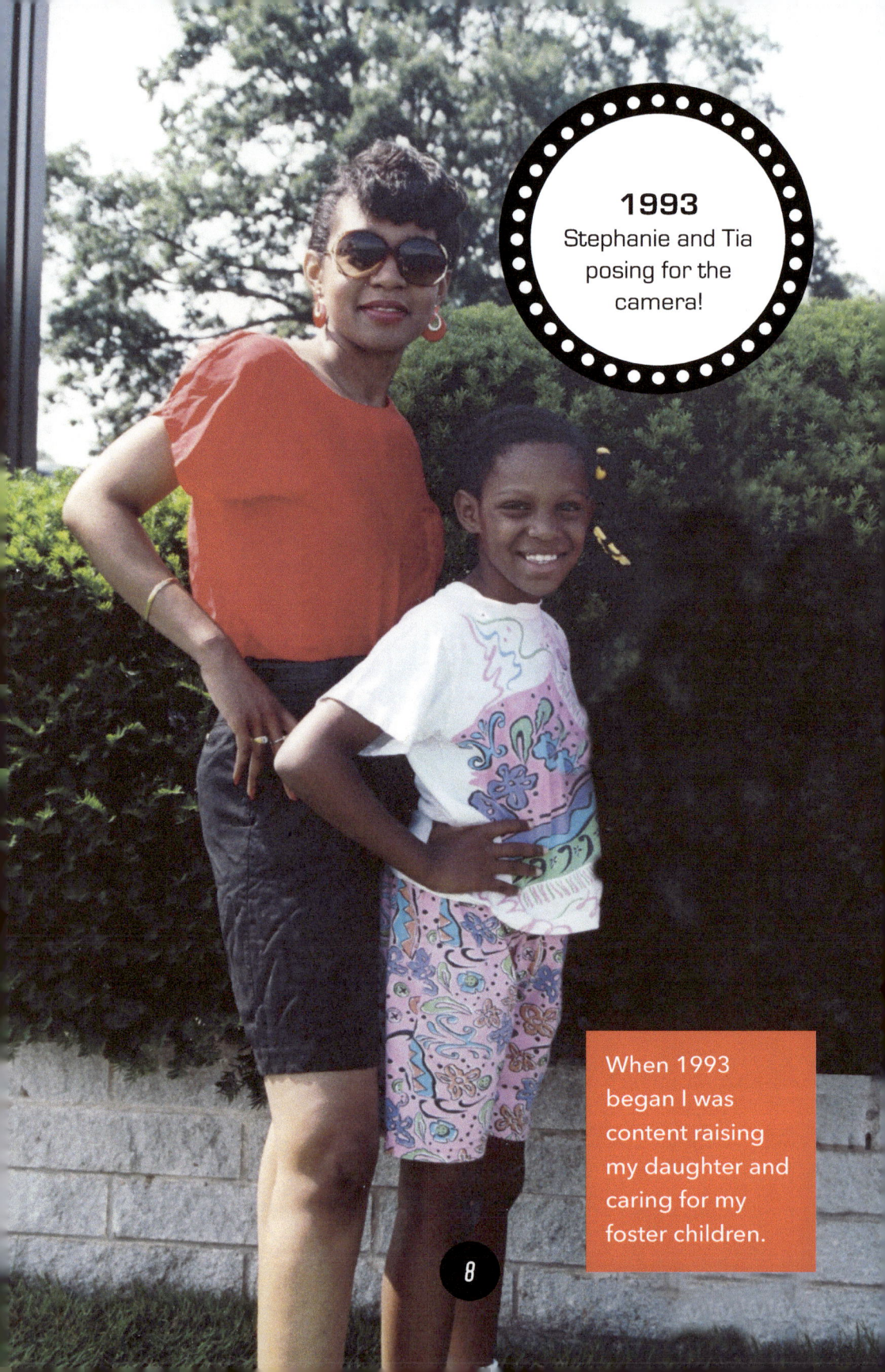

1993
Stephanie and Tia posing for the camera!

When 1993 began I was content raising my daughter and caring for my foster children.

8

When I Met STU
Uncovering the "mystery man"

A new year has always been exciting to me because it brings expectations and possibilities. It is life's do over. January 1st is like having a clean and shiny blank blackboard and several boxes of white dusty chalk in front of us. We just need to take the chalk, get our hands dirty and write something. I had resolved in my heart to make the next 365 days of my the life the best I have ever lived. It is a good feeling when you can say yesterday was good, but today is going to be much better. God has promised us a world of abundance and I am ready to receive the best.

It is five years after my divorce and I no longer have those haunting dreams of a vicious black dog with razor sharp teeth trying to bite me repeatedly. The terrifying dream was symbolic of my nightmare marriage, which is in the distant blurry past. I only talk to my ex-husband during his occasional visitation appointments with our daughter. The scary "dog attack" dreams have changed and are reflective of my new independent confidence. Now when I dream, the black dog that once chased me down is restrained by a very short chain with a tight noose-like collar that has rendered that crazy canine harmless. Even the dog's ferocious bark, which generated deep terror in my soul, now sounds like the whimper of a tiny puppy. I am safe and out of reach.

The year 1993 began with an atmosphere of contentment because not only did I have a new job and a peaceful quiet home, but I was also looking forward to my European vacation in March. My life was wonderful and I did not need or want anything. I was happy and thankful! On a cold winter day, Sunday, January 3, 1993, after returning home from church I received a phone call from the "mystery man", the friend of my co-worker's wife who desperately needed to "get a life". My intention was to meet the "mystery man" with no expectations. I was not looking to date anyone or put energy into a relationship. The phone call was very brief and did not reveal much about the "mystery man" except that his first name was Stewart. After a short introduction of ourselves, we decided that the following Sunday would be our first date — a real "blind date". I had no thoughts of what to expect but I was neither excited or nervous about meeting Stewart. My attitude was neutral.

On Saturday, January 9th I called Stewart to cancel our first meeting. The weekend had not gone well for me and I was not in my normal pleasant mood. A "blind date" at the moment was not at the top of my priority list. Although my expectations were low, I wanted our first meeting to be without distractions. Maybe subconsciously I wanted Stewart to be discouraged, because I was not sure if he would still be interested. Once again our conversation was short and we agreed to delay our date until the following Sunday.

During the next week I occasionally thought about my upcoming date with Stewart, the "mystery man". The thoughts were brief daydreams that evaporated like steam as soon as they crept into my head because the routine of every day life was more important to me than meeting a stranger. After a long work week, Sunday, January 17th finally arrived and it was no different than any other Sunday in the middle of winter. It was a cold blustery day and all I wanted to do was stay inside where it was warm and not venture outside in the frigid temperatures to meet someone that I did not know. Even though I would have rather jumped under a blanket, I decided to keep my commitment and meet Stewart.

Earlier during the week, my mother had agreed to babysit the girls while I was on my date. Sometime plans, even the best plans, can change like the weather in Ohio. The plan was to drop the girls off at my parent's house, but my Mom at the last minute decided that she could not babysit. My parents had become concerned about the "mystery man" and whether it was safe for me to go on a blind date. I did not want to call Stewart and cancel our date again. It was frustrating because I was a grown woman, but my parents were making decisions for me like I was a little lost school girl. Maybe they had visions of me being kidnapped and tied-up in some dark damp basement in an unknown location. This was not my first blind date and I was perfectly comfortable with meeting someone I did not know. At the last moment, my youngest brother Steve decided to watch the girls. This was a small miracle, because Steve had never baby sat for me before. The clock was ticking so loud it was blaring and I needed to get home and get ready for my date.

On the drive home from my parents house I was still gathering my thoughts about meeting someone "new". I was at a point in my life where I was not looking for a husband, not even a boyfriend. During my first marriage I was very naive and can remember "looking for" and asking God for a husband. This resulted in a bad marriage because I was not specific in what I wanted in a loving relationship. At the time I did not adhere to what the bible says about marriage: "He who finds a wife finds a good thing." Now I realize if there is someone (a true soul mate) meant for me, they would have to find me. Although I was not in a hurry, I still prayed that God would some day give me a husband that is wonderful beyond my imagination.

As I arrived at my house, I decided to treat my blind date like a job interview and I wanted my first impression to be good. I was at a place of peace with myself and God. Although I am still not expecting much, I wanted Stewart to see that I was someone special. Inside my closet, I found a nice suit to wear along with matching shoes. I combed my hair until every stray hair was in place. My make-up complimented my clothing and hair in near flawless perfection. I was ready for my "interview/blind date".

I could hear a car in my driveway and soon there was the sound of a door closing. As I began walking to the front door, a series of soft knocks could be heard. I opened the door and a tall African-American man introduced himself as Stewart. He was neatly dressed in a blue jacket, sweater, dark slacks and nice shoes. As we walked to his car, Stewart was a gentleman and opened the passenger door for me. Along the 15 minute ride to a local restaurant, there were exchanges of pleasant small talk. At the restaurant, we were seated by the waitress at a window that faced the west and slowly setting sun. Even though it was very cold, it was a "good" winter day with bright sunshine peaking through some pretty white puffy clouds.

The food and conversation were both plentiful and good. It was easy talking to Stewart because he was down to earth. He genuinely wanted to know about me and did not mind sharing details about himself. During somewhere in the conversation, Stewart became very relaxed and told me that he had holes in the bottom of his shoes and that his feet got wet when it rained. What? Was this a test to make me run to the door and end the date, which to this point had been very good? I actually did not think much about it, because I remember a time in my life when there were holes in my shoes. The "blind date" had actually materialized into a nice evening shared by two people who found a lot in common.

On the way home, we talked more than on the way to the restaurant and we seemed to have more to talk about. Even though our meeting was nice, (especially for a first date), I had no intentions of seeing him again. My life was very comfortable and ridiculously routine — you could almost describe it as boring. It was like watching clothes dry on a clothes line. I had everything I needed and the only thing I lacked was chaos. A lack of chaos was a good thing for me and my girls. Stewart was a nice looking well-mannered man with a good personality and we discovered that we shared a lot in common, but I was not looking for anyone. During our conversation, he may have mentioned he wanted to get married someday in the near future but my ears pretended not to hear him. Once again I thought, I am not looking for a husband.

One thing about Stewart that remained constant throughout the evening was his good manners. It is hard to find a thoughtful individual who actually cares about others and not the selfish inward needs of themselves. He was a genuine gentleman. As we arrived at my house, Stewart walked me to the door, gave me a warm handshake, and then quietly drove away.

The sun setting into the cold winter sky marked an end to a good evening. During the drive to my parents house to pick-up my girls, I reviewed my date with Stewart in my mind several times. My parents, who had tried to discourage me from going on my blind date, were filled with curiosity and asked me immediately about my evening. I think they expected me to say, "You were right , Stewart was a creepy crawly monster and I wish I had not meant him today!" When I told my father and mother that Stewart was a nice gentlemen, I could not tell if they were surprised or disappointed. My father was still concerned and believed it was still too dangerous to go on a blind date. In my daily life I always took precautions and let my family know where I was going, besides I knew God was watching over me. My parents concern was just useless worry, because I had no plans to go on any dates or blind dates in the near future.

The weekend was over and on Monday I returned to work and

like every other Monday before that, I was back to my routine. I thanked Charles for having introduced Stewart to me and let him know that I had a wonderful evening. Charles asked if I had plans on seeing Stewart again, to which I replied, no.

About the middle of the week I found a surprise in my mailbox among the other usual bills and junk mail. Stewart had sent me a thoughtful "homemade" card thanking me for our recent date and his desire to see me again. He really wanted to see me again? The following day, he called and asked me to go out on another date and of course, I was still not interested, and told him I was not available. Prior to our first date, I had grown tired of the dating game. I did not have the desire to devote time to meaningless relationships that brought negative energy to my happy life. Although he was always polite, Stewart was very persistent, (like a solicitor), and called again a couple days later. It seemed like he was going to keep calling until I agreed to see him again. This time, I said I was sick, so I had a good excuse to say no but I was not sure if Stewart believed me. If I were him, I would have probably never called again. I would have taken the hint after the 2nd or 3rd time and just disappeared forever. If I did not know any better, I was starting to think that Stewart was on a mission. Call it "mission Stephanie". Like a consistently ticking clock, Stewart once again called me this time to see how I was feeling but I was still pretending to be sick. He immediately, without skipping a beat, said, "I can bring something over to your house to make you feel better as well as some brownies for the girls." The word no had become a familiar word in my vocabulary, but now I had to say yes this time. After about 90 minutes had passed, there was a soft knock at my door, like there was the first time we met. I opened the door and it was Stewart holding a vase of flowers. The vase was an old 16 oz. Pepsi bottle that was spray painted white. It was unique and pretty. He also brought with him a pan of brownies that were still warm. And that was not all, for my health, Stewart gave me an orange with a decorative gift bow attached. If he was trying to impress me, he did! I invited Stewart to stay and eat some brownies while we watched television. His kindness and caring spirit captured my heart and melted my relenting reluctance. I was ready for his friendship.

Over the next couple of weeks the person I once referred to as the "mystery man" had become a good friend. We enjoyed seeing each other and talking occasionally over the phone. We were building a good foundation in our relationship. When February 14th, Valentines Day, arrived, I did not know what to expect from Stewart. We were friends but this was a romantic holiday. I knew Stewart had a romantic spirit and would not miss giving me something to commemorate the "day of love", so I was a little nervous. He did not disappoint me and arrived at my door with a big gift bag. I reached deep in the gift bag to find a calendar book and a gift card. It was a from a clothing store. More specifically, it was a lingerie store I had never visited before. In only a few weeks I have discovered that Stewart is creative and likes to do things a little different. Along with each gift, there were special instructions for me to follow. For the beautiful calendar, I was instructed to write down anything special about our relationship over the next year. The calendar had plenty of lines and spaces to write, kind of like a diary. The gift card had a higher degree of difficulty. Stewart told me I had to buy something from the lingerie store and model whatever I purchased. At first I was not sure what to think, especially since I had never been to this particular store before. I was raised in the old fashioned church. My roots were conservative down to my underwear. This was exciting and scary at the same time because Christian women, I thought, did not shop in these kinds of places. Then I thought to myself, it is just clothing.

A few days later I went to the "clothing" store. Once inside, I realized that there were many things to buy besides lingerie. Not only was there underwear, but perfumes, lotions and clothing (the outside kind of clothing). It was a refreshing new experience for me. I took my time and carefully picked out an item that I could purchase with my gift card, knowing that I had promised to model whatever I bought for Stewart to see. After a few days I had Stewart come over to my house and ask him to have a seat on the sofa so I could model the gift I had especially selected. He had no idea what I had bought and I was not sure what he expected. We were both like little children anticipating some big magical event. As he sat patiently on the edge of the sofa, I walked into the next room and paused for several minutes (I did this to build the excitement). Just before I returned to the room where Stewart sat patiently waiting, I asked him to close his eyes. As I stepped towards the sofa, I placed my hand in his hand and then had him slowly lift the open side of my wrist to his nose. Stewart opened his eyes and was pleasantly surprised with a beautiful aroma of sweet scented perfume. That is right! I purchased a wonderful bottle of perfume to model. I felt like a whole new world had been born right before my eyes (and nose). I was ready for any new adventure that Stewart and I could share together.

20

■ Valentine's Day 1993

When I Met Stephanie
Uncovering the "mystery woman"

My life could be described as "Happy - Go - Lucky". God has always watched over my family and I even if sometimes I was unaware. The formative years were very pleasant as I replay the 1960s and 1970s in my mind. Those decades have melted away except for the images that entertain nostalgic trivia with my memory. Even if my recollection is not quite accurate about a certain past event, I always have a sense of contentment and happiness concerning my childhood. We had a small family that consisted of my Dad, Mom, brother (Vincent) and myself. Vincent and I shared some of the same artistic and music talents that allowed us to participate in many activities together. We were good friends who understood each other. My Mom always said we were psychic twins. Sometimes she would take us aside separately and asked us to pick clothes out of a catalog for one another. Each time, with almost 100% accuracy, we would pick the same exact item on the same page. While at the University of Dayton, I took a Philosophy class that Vincent had taken the previous school semester. The professor was amazed that I selected the very same seat, even though I was unaware of where my brother sat or even that he took the same class. We were close.

Although I would illustrate my childhood as happy one, there were a few times when the picture was not perfect. My Mom and Dad separated when I was about nine years old. It was for the best because my parents were not getting along and their decaying relationship affected the atmosphere of the entire house. In 1969, it was very common (especially in our neighborhood) for woman to stay at home and raise their children, but my Mom as a result of the separation had to go back to work. This was just before the 1970s and all of our friend's mothers did not work outside the home. It was just as uncommon to live in a separated or divorced home. I can remember one of my friends saying, "Your Daddy ran away from your Mommy." There was definitely a social stigma attached to homes without two parent's decades ago. I believe there was only one television show in the 1960s, "Julia", that addressed a single parent household. Single parent homes were perceived as different, chaotic and without discipline. Vincent and I were given freedom but with an understanding of boundaries and rules. We were not perfect but I believe in most cases, we had more discipline than most of our friends who had both parents at home. My Mom always said that one good parent is better than two so-so parents. She did an excellent job of raising my brother and I in a loving home without Daddy. Our lives were stable to a maddening degree. We lived in the same house, went to one elementary school and one high school our entire childhood. The stability was not boring. Stability gave us great peace and a sense of belonging especially after Mom and Dad broke up. We were connected.

Without a little risk, humans are destined to a stale existence with little chance of growth or opportunity. In November of 1992, I was living a life of routine beyond extraordinary proportions. Work, work, and more work. Sometimes I would compile as many as 70 hours of work in a work week. I really enjoyed my job as a graphic designer. Ever since I was a child, I always enjoyed anything related to art, especially if it involved any kind of drawing. My father was a Technical Illustrator at Wright Patterson Air Force Base and I was never very far from his drawing table, which was usually covered with drawings. My hobbies as a youngster had materialized into a full-time occupation complete with pay and benefits. The only one glaring issue was that my life was very methodical with no variety in any sense. I lived by myself in a big two story house with only the bark of my mixed Lab, Corey, to keep me company. On occasion, I would date in between all the work hours, but no significant relationships ever developed. There was never a genuine connection. My heart desired a real change or strategy toward relationships. My co-workers were always trying to fix me up with someone they knew. Blind dates were scary in some aspects but also allowed a sense of non-attachment to any possible relationship. If the dates were bad, then I did not feel obligated because I did not choose this particular person. I could always blame the matchmaker, when it did not work out and almost 100% of time these dates resulted in "plane-nose diving" failure. Against the approval of some of my friends and co-workers I enlisted the help of the Personal Ads. You know the ads in which most people are known to stretch the truth about themselves especially concerning physical aspects and education. In essence, this was a blind date based upon a personal resume. At least in this case, I was making my own selection, even if it was a selection based upon exaggerated personal information. Maybe, I should have listened to my friends. The series of dates I went on in November of 1992 were nothing short of catastrophic disasters. If it is true that everyone has a person specifically made for them, then I managed to find every person in the world not made for me. It is like putting a fish and cat together. Sure there is an odd curiosity, but eventually the cat will eat the fish. At the time, it was probably in my best interest and survival on earth to take a break from dating. I am certain my friends and co-workers were exhausted listening to endless "train wreck" stories. There was a bright side. I was still breathing and my dog did not have any fleas.

In late December of 1992, all my co-workers had heard about my dating failures and given up on helping me. My abilities of persuasiveness had vanished along with the last bad date. I could not sell a coffin to a dead man. There were several question marks flashing in my mind. Was it easier for me to start a good relationship or catch a goldfish in the ocean? Odds were that I needed a fishing pole and some good bait. The task appeared to be daunting and extremely bleak. But sometimes we must try again until all possible avenues have been exhausted. Success can be just a few feet from your last failure. What if I had given up while learning to ride my bike as a child? Do they make training wheels for a 200 pound grown man? It is not something you would wish to see, except maybe at a circus where clowns with big rubber shoes drive tiny small toy cars. In the real world, we have to get back up on the bike and try again without a safety net or the fake attachable nose. Reality has to make sense. Even after watching me crash and burn on several occasions, there was one co-worker who still had faith and was brave enough to shift through the mangled wreckage. Her name was Rosemary. I had worked with Rosemary for almost a year and found her to be very pleasant and positive. One day Rosemary asked if I was interested in meeting someone. She explained that her husband worked with a nice lady who was single. Wait a minute! This sounds like another blind date disaster waiting to happen. I was immediately hesitant, but at the same time I expected something wonderful because of Rosemary's great spirit. It seemed like a reasonable risk. So I asked Rosemary to get a phone number via her husband. On January 3, 1993, I called Stephanie for the first time. I hardly ever used the phone unless I was ordering pizza. Just dialing Stephanie's number was a major event, because I have never been comfortable talking on the phone. Our conversation, which only lasted for a few minutes, was pleasantly friendly. Before saying goodbye, we arranged to meet the following Sunday afternoon for dinner. As I started the work week, my spirit filled with anticipation about seeing Stephanie in person. The only other time in my life I could remember that same feeling of excitement was on Christmas Day when I was a child. On Christmas Eve, I could hardly sleep without thinking about the surprises that were neatly hidden under the tree. My patience level was similar to that of a little kid's, but I had enough restraint or common sense not to show up at Stephanie's door at five in the morning. The wait for our "big date" was a little longer because Stephanie called to reschedule for the following Sunday. When January 17th finally arrived, it was a typical crisp winter day with deep blue skies and puffy clouds. Stephanie was brave enough to allow me to pick her up at her residence even though I was a stranger. I could have been a serial killer and now I know where she lives, or more likely a loser who now knows where she lives. Now I know possibly one of two things about Stephanie. #1) - she is completely crazy and would not care if a serial killer appeared at her doorstep or #2) - she is very careless. Stephanie's bravery actually stimulated my curiosity and added to the unexplainable excitement of the day ahead. As Stephanie opened the door, I was pleasantly relieved that she was from the planet Earth and not a creepy critter on the Sci-Fi channel. For a blind date, this is a very good start. She is not only attractive but she is very tall. First impressions are lasting and I was overwhelmingly stunned by Stephanie's beauty. We arrived at a local restaurant and were seated near the windows on the west side of dining area. The afternoon sun, which was rare on a winter day in January, playfully peaked through large beautiful clouds and filtered through the window blinds. Billowing steam from chimneys on buildings nearby was the only indication of the freezing temperatures. This was not your typical winter day or typical blind date. On a blind date, the conversation usually is very awkward and strained. Talking to your dentist, with a mouth full of gauze, during an annual check-up would prove an easier task. Stephanie and I were as comfortable as old school buddies at a high school reunion. The conversation flowed in many different streams as we shared our experiences and goals for the future.

Talking to Stephanie was like talking to a reflection of myself. We had much in our lives that was common and familiar. How do you know when you are comfortable with someone you just met? The answer is when you say, "The soles of my shoes have holes resulting in damp feet during rainfall." What would possess anyone to allow damaging confidential information to be shared with a stranger? It seemed like I was programmed to sabotage the outcome of my date, considering my most recent attempts at a relationship were disastrous. Fortunately, Stephanie seemed to be amused by my "humbleness" or lack of quality shoe-ware. The good news was that the weather forecast did not include any liquid or frozen precipitation. I immediately knew that Stephanie's beauty emanated from her center and was not just a skin deep facade.

Stephanie was an intelligent person with a positive attitude toward life and was unlike any of my recent dates. As I drove Stephanie home and the wonderful afternoon came to an end, I internally wished for a second date. Did I believe in love at first sight? Not really. My philosophy was that anything with worth or value took time to develop, including relationships. On television, we are constantly delivered the illusion or hallucination that two people can fall madly in love in a thirty minute program (including commercials). It is about the same amount of time it takes to make instant potatoes by just adding water. Some things in life do not require much thought but a meaningful relationship needs to be nurtured. In a Corvette, you can drive from 0 to 60 mph in a few seconds without breaking a bead of sweat, but a quality friendship requires real effort and commitment. Stephanie was an unique gem in a sea of common gravel. I was genuinely intrigued as I anticipated the opportunity to build a new friendship. Although it was only a brief encounter on a cold winter day, Stephanie's essence quickly echoed through my soul like a warm summer breeze blowing across the Gulf of Mexico. I felt connected.

MAGIC ON FILM

From the time I met Stephanie, I was always fascinated with her outward beauty — over time I realized it was her giant heart that was shining through. Maybe this is why I have taken so many photos of her over the years — just trying to capture the magic of her kind spirit. The following pages display a few of those pics... ⇨

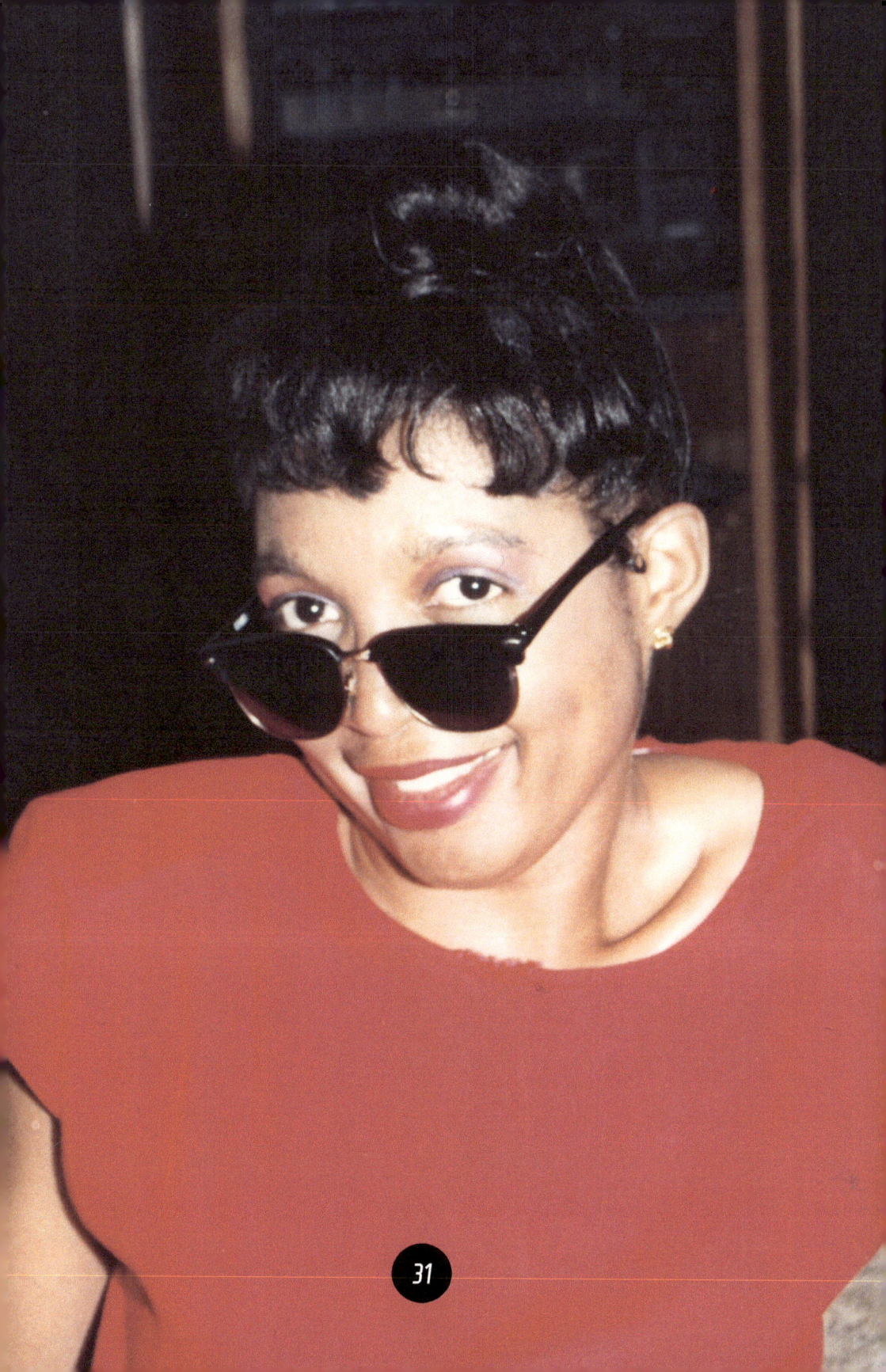

34

One + One + One =
Instant family

There were big changes in my life in less than a year. Stephanie and I were engaged to be married on September 17, 1993, after eight months of dating. I am now on the verge of going from Mr. Solo to Mr. Family Man with a family composed of Stephanie and Tia. I was a little apprehensive of becoming a husband and father all in the blink of an eye — after all I had never been a husband or a parent — but I also knew my love for Stephanie and her daughter would overcome any of life's obstacles.

I remember seeing the first episode of the "Brady Bunch", when Carol (with her three daughters) married Mike (with his three sons + Tiger, the dog). The show was a cliché of instant conflict displaying what happens when "strangers" come together. It was a 30 minute TV show and the conflicts disappeared after that episode. Real life does not work that way — it takes time and patience to develop a relationship, especially between an adult and a child. I never liked the term "step-father". I know Tia had a father, but I knew I could also be a father — and I wanted to be there for her. Our relationship was not always the best, but over time I have come to love Tia very much — sometimes good things just take a little time — she is my daughter.

■ Family photo taken in 1994 prior to wedding

We Got Married!
September 17, 1994

WEDDING OUTTAKE

A long story, but this photo was taken in 1993 while planning the wedding. The only dress that survived the cut was the one being worn by Steph's sister Karen on the right.

Off to The honeymoon!

Two days after getting married we headed off to our honeymoon — a four day cruise to Key West and Cozumel, Mexico on board Carnival Ecstasy. This was our first cruise, so we had no idea what to expect or what to do sometimes. One night when we had re-boarded the ship after visiting the port of call, Cozumel, missing our dinner time in the dining room — we were starving! We could have ordered room service, but we thought we had to pay a large fee and did not realize room service was free. We went to bed "dreaming" about food. It really did not matter because we were happy experiencing new adventures together.

HAPPY!
We are enjoying the last night of our first cruise!

Family is Everything —
Growing Together

Twenty-five years ago at the beginning of our union, it was just three of us — Stu + Steph + Tia. On a cold blustery winter day in January of 1996, the twins, Veronica and Victoria entered our world. I know what you are thinking — a house full of women and one bathroom — somehow we made it work. The small details or inconveniences really are trivial when you have the love and support of your family. No matter what our busy daily schedules included, we always would sit down for dinner together — an old tradition that is not practice as much in today's hectic non-stop world. Another tradition we have kept over the years is attending the University of Dayton Alumni Bandcoming every fall with my brother Vincent. Traditions bring us together to connect and experience something as a group — building memories that always stay in our spirits.

Every year I create a custom Christmas card, another family tradition, (which includes a family photo) that I send out to hundreds of friends and family members — just another way we stay connected. It is amazing to see how much our family has grown, matured and changed over the many years. In February 2015, our family portrait changed that year when Tia gave birth to our first grandchild, Antwan Dale Halfacre Tucker — yes, finally another male to even the odds. He is an energetic and smart little boy. Another addition to our portrait is Victoria's doggie, Luna (a sweet Pit Bull) that reminds me of my old dog, Corey, just reverse coloring. I have to admit it has been a challenge photographing a little boy and a dog together in the same session, but somehow it always works out in the end.

We are proud of all three daughters and know they will continue to pursue their dreams and make a positive impact on the world. I hope we have set an example of working hard, being kind to others and living a life of integrity — just making a practice of doing the right thing. My Mom's favorite saying was, "It does not hurt to be kind." Proudly I can say that those sentiments have been exhibited by Tia, Veronica or Victoria on many occasions involving their family and friends.

Thank you God for our family — we are grateful!

2018
Christmas card
photo shoot at
Eastwood Park.

HALFACRE FAMILY

■ Photo taken on 2017 family cruise

2015
One of our favorite Christmas card covers. Poor Antwan was so cold.

A Beautiful Journey
Stu's perspective

The past twenty-five years with Stephanie have been the best years of my life. Have we changed — the answer is yes. Our relationship has become richer over time because we appreciate each other and most importantly remain best friends. I just enjoy being in her presence and talking or taking a walk together. As much as we are alike, we also have different perspectives and opinions on some things. The reason I believe our relationship is successful is because we work hard at making it work. Anything in life that is good can not survive without continuous effort.

We have experienced some great times but also difficult periods together. It hurt me when Stephanie had to go through painful breast cancer surgeries and physically/mentally challenging chemotherapy treatments. I am happy that I was there to help her through her daily fight. What I learned during those tough times was how strong her faith really was — she never lost her faith or let her spirit get crushed. Even when struggling with the treatments, she still took time to be there for family and friends. I admire Stephanie and will love her always and forever!

I know there is a God, because HE made her especially for me.

A Beautiful Journey
Steph's perspective

It's been 25 wonderful years of marriage with my best friend, Stewart. I remember when I first met Stu, he only attended church four times a year — Easter, Mother's Day, Thanksgiving and Christmas. Later in our marriage he began going to help me carry our twin daughters up the hill to the front entrance of the church. One day he testified that he had been in church for ten weeks straight. My thought was whose counting – he was, lol. Now it's 25 years later, and he is still in church.

Our relationship has grown over the years with ups and downs. Stu's father, who I never had the chance to meet, passed away a few days before my trip to Germany in March 1993. In September 2009, the loss of his mom was very hard. Stu learned from her death how to eat right. Like his mom Stu had become a diabetic. He worked hard to change his diet and reversed the effects of his diabetes. As a result of learning how to cook healthier meals he was a great help when I was diagnosed with breast cancer. The healthy meals that Stu prepared were beneficial in my long healing process. I rarely got sick during my chemotherapy treatments. Stu was my support and anchor. I thank God that he was there by my side through the sleepless nights and long days.

The "walking man still" managed to take his walks and maintain the house, while caring for my needs. I will forever be grateful for his loving and caring heart.

Stu has been my support person from the first day I met him. He is always supportive of my ideas and dreams. He said I dressed like the girls from Little House on the Prairie — so he enjoys buying clothes and making me his fashion plate. I believe he should have been a clothing designer because of his good taste in clothes.

We were both surprised when our oldest daughter Tia said she was changing her last name officially to Halfacre. This is a testimony of what a great man he is. He is a great father and husband and friend.

My motto for our marriage has always been — I thank God for yesterday and today and I pray that tomorrow will be just as nice or better.

Stu and I like spending time with each other walking, relaxing in the park or just sitting on the bed watching Netflix movies. We enjoy our quiet time together to talk or just hold hands. We both enjoy traveling and spending time with family and friends.

THE 25TH ANNIVERSARY TRIP!

For our anniversary we wanted to do something special and memorable. Our honeymoon was our first time on a cruise and we really enjoyed it. Since 1994 we experienced six more cruises (some with the family). So for our 8th cruise we booked an eight day adventure aboard the Carnival Horizon out of Miami, FL. We arrived in Ft. Lauderdale and stayed in Miami Beach across from the ocean the day before sailing. The ship (with 4000 passengers) had port of calls in the southern Caribbean - Grand Turk, Dominican Republic, Curacao, and Aruba – all beautiful places surrounded by an amazing and vast ocean. After the cruise returned to Miami, we stayed one more day in Ft. Lauderdale across from the beach before heading home. It was the best vacation we have ever taken and a great way to celebrate 25 years of "Love and Happiness".

South Miami Beach Florida

On board Carnival Horizon

Grand Turk

Curacao

Aruba

62

Aruba

Last days at sea

Ft Lauderdale Florida

On November 17, 2019, our beautiful daughters organized a 25th anniversary party for us!

SCAN QR CODE TO SEE MORE PHOTOS ➔

Thanks for Your Love and Support!

To all our family and friends who have been in our lives the past 25 years, we thank you! All relationships benefit from the love and support of others. Life over the past quarter century has been richer because you were a part of it. Many blessings and love.

In Remembrance

To the many family & friends that are gone
but remain in our hearts always...

Walter Halfacre
(Father)

Jollis Welcher
(Uncle)

LaVerne Halfacre
(Mother)

Paul Welcher
(Uncle)

Consuelo Velar
(Grandmother)

Yvonne "Molly" Welcher
(Aunt)

Sadie Wilson
(Grandmother)

Janis "Cookie" Welcher
(Cousin)

Fred Wilson
(Grandfather)

Dorismarie Welcher
(Cousin)

Ophelia Wilson
(Aunt)

Margaret McKinney
(Grandmother)

Jerry Napier
(Cousin)

Howard McKinney
(Uncle)

Sheila Wilson
(Sister-in-law)

Jimmy McKinney
(Uncle)

Rosetta Appleberry
(Aunt)

Jake McKinney
(Uncle)

Charles Dannin
(Friend/Matchmaker)

Bill Johnson
(Friend)

Twila Norman
(Aunt)

Mary Louise Wilson
(Mother)

www.ingramcontent.com/pod-product-compliance
Lightning Source LLC
LaVergne TN
LVHW072328080426
835509LV00033B/142